PICTURES THAT PREACH

PICTURES
THAT PREACH

BY
CHARLES NELSON PACE

THE ABINGDON PRESS
NEW YORK   CINCINNATI

Copyright, 1924, by
CHARLES NELSON PACE

Printed in the United States of America

TO MY SON
ROBERT

PICTURES AND PREACHMENT

PICTURES THAT PREACH

THE story is told that when Munkacsy's "Christ Before Pilate" was on exhibition a few years ago in Hamilton, Ontario, a sailor from one of the lake boats accosted the woman who was in attendance at the door with the blunt question,

"Is Christ here? How much to see Christ?"

When he was told the admission fee, he growled out, "Well, I suppose I'll have to pay it," and putting down a piece of silver he swaggered into the room. He sat down in front of the great picture and studied it for a moment or two, and presently off came his hat. He gazed upon it a little longer, and then, leaning down, he picked up the descriptive catalogue which he had dropped when he took his seat. He read it over, and studied the painting anew, dropping his face into his hands at intervals. Thus he remained for a full hour. When he came out there were tears in his eyes, and suppressed sobs in his voice as he said,

"Madam, I came here to see Christ because my mother asked me to. I am a rough man sailing on the lakes, and before I went on this cruise my mother wanted me to see this picture, and I came to please her. I never believed in any such thing, but the man who could paint a picture like that—he must have believed in it. There is something in it that makes me believe in it too."

At the time of the French Revo-

lution a mob swept through the
Tuileries bent upon loot and pillage.
Suddenly they came upon a picture
of Christ—and then turned back.
Such was the arresting power of a
picture.

"There is not a picture on your
walls to indicate whether you are
a Christian or a pagan," said the
father of G. Campbell Morgan to
him, on visiting the home of the son
shortly after his marriage. The
young man corrected this defect.
How revealing the pictures in a
home are!

A mother visited her son in the
dormitory of a great university.
Some of the pictures she found in
his room made her inwardly grieve.
"May I put a picture on your
wall?" she asked. Then she secured
a noble picture of the Christ and

hung it there. The next time she visited him every questionable picture had been removed. "You see," the boy said, "it didn't seem quite right to have them when His picture was hanging there!"

A family that lived inland sent every son to sea. Neither the father nor the mother had ever seen the ocean. It was regarded as a strange thing that their sons should seek lives of adventure so far away from home. Then some one discovered the explanation. Over the fireplace in the home had hung through all the years a magnificent picture of the ocean with its voyaging ships. Evidently, the picture was responsible for the life decisions of these lads.

"Do you see the angel faces all around that picture?" said an old man employed at the Denver University, through whose kindness I was permitted to see the interior of the chapel, at vacation time, in the front of which hangs a wonderful reproduction of the Sistine Madonna. "I looked at that picture a good many times before I saw those angel faces. Then someone pointed them out to me. Now I always see them when I look at that painting. It makes a different picture of it." For many others the picture has been made to live with new meaning because of those angel faces. Pictures in churches may be used as an aid to devotion.

Painters preach. The preacher will be glad for every message that strengthens and enforces the truth he is sent to proclaim. He will call to his assistance every ally—books, science, travel, art.

PICTURES THAT PREACH

There is no visitor in the world's art galleries but that has been impressed by the devotion of art to religion. Here he will find dramatic incidents from the Scriptures and life. Many artists have felt the call to service as truly as any preacher has felt the call of God. It were well therefore to have some acquaintance with their work, feel the fellowship of their motives and call them to the assistance of the church in its proclamation of the gospel message.

Recently this preacher has found it helpful to present picture sermons. We have heard much of book sermons, and they are valuable. We have known of expository and topical sermons. The suggestion of picture sermons is not meant as a substitution for any other kind, and they are not offered as something new under the sun. They mean, so far as this volume is concerned, the use of a great picture as a theme, and a discussion of the theme the picture sets forth. They are not an appreciation of the picture primarily but a presentation of the gospel message contained in the picture. Thus the picture supplements the sermon. It appeals to the eye as well as the ear. It has been our custom to furnish members of the congregation good prints of the picture under discussion and when possible to have a fine copy of it in sight of the whole congregation. Such a picture can often be obtained from the art department of a good store, and on more than one occasion this has been displayed in the window the week preceding it, with the announcement that it was to be a sermon theme the next Sunday night. The prints distributed help to enforce the message, awaken a new appreciation for the picture itself, and are often cherished later and given a place on the walls of humble homes.

"I never knew there was so much to that picture—it will never be the same to me again," said a man after hearing a discussion in which "The Angelus" was the topic. "I had often seen this picture and knew in a general way it was a religious theme, but it will always have a new and wonderful meaning for me from this time." Such testimony becomes current conversation when pictures are used to carry the Master's message to human hearts.

This method is only one of many

that can be used to help interest
people in the church. Is that important? It is of primary importance. We have become accustomed
to say worship is a means to an
end, likewise Sunday and the church
itself. But in these days with multi-
tudinous counter attractions perhaps it were well to make them an
end in themselves. To have a congregation is an achievement. No
man should be satisfied to face
empty seats on Sunday. They do
not glorify God. They publish the
fact that the church is not function-
ing to its capacity. If our times
contain forces that are in competition
with the worship of the church and
tend to diminish the size of congregations then it is necessary to
face that fact with frankness and
devise some way of making the

sermons more interesting and the
worship of God's house more attractive. It does no good to complain
or despair. The suggestion of these
picture sermons is meant to be a
contribution to this problem.

Jesus preached in pictures. He
used symbols constantly. He told
stories. Religious truth was presented in a new and fascinating
form. Men went away in astonish-
ment at what they heard. Their
interest was awakened. Jesus was
not indifferent to public opinion.
He asked his disciples what people
were saying. "Whom do men say
that I am?" He knew you could
not move people until their interest
was captured. The unconvention-
ality with which he preached—by
a well-curb, on a mountain side,
along a lake shore—doubtless was

as sensational to them as what he said.

If one needs a precedent for undertaking to arouse **people**, to arrest attention, to challenge interest, to secure a following, he need go no further than the ministry of Jesus.

Something of this anxiety to get a hearing for God's message must perpetually move the preacher's heart. If old methods do not work, why not try something new? If opening the doors and ringing the bell do not bring the people to church, wringing your hands in discouragement will not do it.

Paul thanked God that even those who opposed Christ unwittingly preached him. "So that in every way Christ is preached" was his motive. The minister has no monopoly on preaching nowadays. Editors preach. Speakers at luncheon clubs often preach. Men in public life preach, for it is noticeable that more and more political questions are moral questions. Movies preach —a few of them. This is not an occasion for resentment but rejoicing. Let us be glad that in so many ways God's message of truth, justice, brotherhood, and good will is being declared. It were well also to remember that this condition imposes added responsibilities on the pulpit. A preacher's barrel in these days is good for nothing but kindling wood. Preparing to preach would seem to be something more than consultation of a commentary. The services at church need not be pokey in order to be pious. Diversity of program, the use of light and color and good music, the effort

to interest people, that you may
win them for Christ and his kingdom, are all a part of the preparation for Sunday. To fill the house
of God with people is one step
toward filling it with God's glory.
To awaken their laughter or tears
may be a means of arousing their
conscience. To attract them by
lifting religion into the region of
good cheer, of romance, of beauty,
of heroic service has power to make
indifferent people different.

The fact that many pastors, learning of these picture sermons, have
made inquiries concerning them, has
led to the preparation of this book.
It is hoped it may help a great
many churches.

It need scarcely be said the author
does not profess to be an art critic.
He undertakes to be primarily a

preacher of the gospel and has always been eager for any help he could secure to illuminate and enforce his Master's message. The picture sermons presented in brief outline here were preached to congregations that filled a great auditorium and grew out of a sustained evangelistic desire which in eight years has added more than two thousand to the membership of the church.

THE SISTINE MADONNA   Raphael

THE SISTINE MADONNA

IF the soul may be regarded as a city with walls and gates from which we send our embassies of influence and our marching armies of speech, then it is through the eye-gate that much of the tribute is brought to enrich the treasury of the inner life. We are told that about eighty per cent of the information we obtain comes through the power of vision. "What went ye out for to see," Jesus asked the multitude. It expresses an attitude toward life. Those who teach us to see that which is beautiful in nature and eternal in the realms of truth render a real service. It has been given to some with immortal genius to catch these visions of splendor and spread them upon the canvas where they have remained to bless mankind. Such pictures enrich the world and preach perpetually.

Travelers in Europe who come to Dresden will find that here art is supreme. In the Royal Gallery are many treasures of surpassing value, the lovely work of vision-led men. Raphael's masterpiece, "The Sistine Madonna," is to be found in this gallery. It was originally painted for a church in the village of Piacenza, Italy. Now it occupies a room by itself in this famous center of art. It is a symphony in color. It casts a spell upon the beholder that subdues and quiets. It invokes reverence and prayer. Voices in this room are seldom raised above a whisper. It is as though one visited a shrine. Those who come to admire remain to worship.

What is the message of this great picture?

1. It illustrates the preservative power of religion. Raphael lived in a period of intellectual awakening. Invention and discovery were quickening the life of the world. It was a time of expanding frontiers. Caxton built his printing press in England. The first watch was made at Nuremberg. Columbus set sail and discovered America. Lorenzo de' Medici filled all Florence with his name and fame as the patron of art and letters; and there too Savonarola denounced the corruptions of church and state. It was the time of the Spanish inquisition and Portugal's golden age. It was the era in which Michael Angelo lived—

and to be a contemporary artist with him were somewhat of a distinction. The fifteenth century is one of the most notable in the Christian era.

But back of all these activities was a religious motive. Caxton built his press in order that the Bible might be printed. Columbus sailed westward in the hope that he might win converts to the cross as well as to find a waterway to India. Michael Angelo wrought on Saint Peter's Cathedral. In a similar way the artist Raphael was moved by spiritual impulse. The work which these did has entered into the religious heritage of the world. Is it not interesting to discover that those whose names still live from that distant date are those who connected their lives, their genius, their talents, and their services with the kingdom of God? Their work is imperishable because they jo ned it to an imperishable cause.

"All passes—Art alone remains" is a quotation to be seen above the door of the Fine Arts Building in Chicago. Without entering upon a controversy in this matter we know that some things do pass away and some things have power to abide. The practical question to each one of us is, "Do you want your life to count? Do you want your services to be cherished after you are dead?" "Be ye steadfast, unmovable, always abounding in the work of the Lord, forasmuch as ye know that your labor is not in vain in the Lord." "There shall never be one lost good," declared Browning. God is anxious to build his kingdom in the world and would seem to be eager to lay hold of each human service that will contribute to this end. Because Raphael sought to glorify God in the painting of his picture it has come to a place in the world's life that survives the passing centuries.

2. This picture also suggests the ministry of a little child. Critics have said that the artist sought to express in the figures which are here presented the cardinal virtues of faith, hope and love. Saint Sixtus is the embodiment of hope and he looks with eagerness to Christ as he points to a needy world. Saint Barbara, with face averted from the glory of this divine revelation, and kneeling, expresses the attitude of love. The cherubs recall, "Inasmuch as ye did it not to one of the

least of these." Mary and her Child in sacred relationship portray faith. It is not blind and unintelligent faith, but one which is open-eyed, honest, and ready to accept the commission of God to a waiting world.

When Jesus "set a child in their midst," he expressed the genius of Christianity. The training of the child-life of any generation is not only the most statesmanlike procedure for securing the spread of faith, but the spirit of a little child is the qualification for discipleship. One of the most encouraging things in our modern church life is the attention which is being paid to the children. Wonderful results have been achieved not only in the moral instruction of youth but in such practical matters as sanitation, pre-

natal care, and the service of visiting nurses. When we learn that
Robert Burns had nine children,
most of whom died in infancy, and
that Samuel Wesley was the father
of nineteen, and that when John,
the fifteenth child, was born there
were but six other children in the
family, one cannot help but wonder
what the world has lost through
this infant mortality. How different
it is to-day! In the Near-East and
in Europe we are trying to save the
children. In our own country,
schools and hospitals, playgrounds
and Juvenile Courts, the Big Brother
movement, and the care of the
underprivileged child are all expres-
sions of this Christian impulse to
save the coming generation. It were
well to challenge men of affairs with
the gospel message and remember

that the appeal of the cross has a power to save unto the uttermost all who come. But in saving the child to Christian life and service we are helping to shape the destiny of the world to Christian ideals.

3. This picture suggests the mystery of incarnation. This mystery is delicately suggested in a recent poem:

"A tired old doctor died to-day and a baby
    boy was born—
A little new soul that was pink and frail,
    and a soul that was gray and worn.
And—half-way here and half-way there
On a white, high hill of shining air—
They met and passed and paused to speak
    in the flushed and hearty dawn.

"The man looked down at the soft, small
    thing, with wise and weary eyes,
And the little chap stared back at him with
    startled, scared surmise,
And then he shook his downy head—

33

'I think I won't be born,' he said.
'You are too gray and sad!' He shrank
   from the pathway down the skies.

"But the tired old doctor roused once more
   at the battle-cry of birth,
And there was memory in his look, of grief
   and toil and mirth.
'Go on!' he said. 'It's good—and bad:
It's hard! *Go on!* It's *ours*, my lad.'
He stood and urged him out of sight, down
   to the waiting earth."

Raphael's picture expresses that
dramatic moment when the veil between heaven and earth has been
parted. The curtains are drawn
aside and Mother and Child are
looking out upon the world with
wonder, amazement, and surprise.
All the critics give Raphael the
credit for having painted the most
wonderful Christ-child to be found
upon any canvas. There is in the

face a combination of that which is human and divine. It is infancy with distinction. It is the same face that Hofmann later painted in the pictures of "Christ in the Temple" and "The Rich Young Ruler" but grown older with the passing years. In Raphael's conception it is as though the mystery of his mission had just broken across their consciousness. It is as though they were appalled by the awaiting task. They come—these two, Mother and Child—treading on diaphanous clouds with angel faces innumerable about them, recalling the Scripture, "Which things the angels desire to look into," the splendors of heaven pouring its radiance upon the earth.

What is the spiritual significance of this to us? "The Word was made flesh, and dwelt among us."

God became man that men might learn to live in a godlike way. He took residence on the earth that earth might be more like heaven. He showed us that the flesh need not be a devilish thing but full of grace and truth.

But this historic event is the symbol of a process. It is ever God's purpose that the Word shall be made flesh, that the physical shall be filled with his glory, that truth shall connect with life, that virtue shall get into action and conduct, that the world shall be a continual incarnation of spiritual forces in human form. God writes his truth not in flaming letters on the sky, nor does he cast them in bronze or chisel them in marble for the guidance of the race. He writes his truth in human life. "I beseech

you therefore, brethren, by the mer-
cies of God, that ye present your
bodies a living sacrifice, holy, acceptable unto God, which is your reason-
able service. And be not conformed
to this world: but be ye transformed
by the renewing of your mind, that
ye may prove what is that good,
and acceptable, and perfect will of
God."

"Take my life, and let it be
Consecrated, Lord, to thee;
Take my moments and my days;
Let them flow in ceaseless praise;
Take my hands, and let them move
At the impulse of thy love;
Take my feet, and let them be
Swift and beautiful for thee."

THE DESCENT FROM THE CROSS

As the traveler approaches the city of Antwerp he beholds the beautiful spire of Notre Dame. It rises in a series of pinnacles two hundred and ten feet high, and from within a hundred bells chime forth the call to prayer. It is a cathedral magnificent in its proportions and elaborate in its decorations. It has stood through centuries like a mighty sentinel while the tides of human life have washed its foundations.

Within Notre Dame hangs Rubens' picture, "The Descent from the Cross." The original sketch of this picture is practically unknown to the world. It is owned by A.

Rubens

THE DESCENT FROM THE CROSS

DESCENT FROM THE CROSS

L. Nicholson, of London. It is a panel forty-five by thirty inches in size and was painted in 1610, while the altar-piece in Notre Dame was painted some years afterward. Those who have compared the two declare that the original is in every way a more brilliant piece of work. Contrasts are seen in the delineation of feature, the soft, lustrous folds of garments, the expression in the eyes of those who appear upon the canvas. The breathless anxiety over the descent of the precious body of Christ as it is taken from the cross is delineated. None who see the great picture at Notre Dame, however, will be disappointed in its magnificent proportions or the splendor of its work. It is one of a series of pictures done by the artist covering the last hours of Jesus' life.

PICTURES THAT PREACH

One feels the realism of these paintings to the point of suffering. It is interesting to know that Rubens used his family and his friends as models for this painting. The artist Van Dyke is portrayed as Zachias, and his pupil Jordans appears as Nicodemus. The Mayor of Antwerp is painted as Joseph of Arimathæa. The women who are portrayed are those of his own family. It is said that the portrait of John is the only one drawn from imagination. The "Descent from the Cross" is one of the most famous paintings in the world. It is fitting that it should hang in a place of worship where it preaches in words of color, in paragraphs of pigments, in an eloquence of mute magnificence the tragic story of the supreme event in human history.

DESCENT FROM THE CROSS

What do we see in this picture?

1. The end of a perfect life. It were as though Jesus had just said, "It is finished." This expiring utterance of the Master seems to linger upon the canvas. What did he mean? Evidently he felt that his mission on earth was finished. From his first recorded utterance, "I must be about my Father's business," until this last, "It is finished," one can draw the straight line of obedience, a life in which there was no deviation, no defect.

We catch now and then a fleeting vision of the life we wish to lead. We hear some lost chord we vainly seek to reproduce in the symphony of our souls. None of us can hope for such a record. We strive for perfection in the realm of learning and commerce. We seek

it in the achievements of our moral
life. If we were to inquire why we
find perfection always eluding us,
Browning would say,

"Ask that particular devil
  Whose task it is to trip the all but at
  Perfection—stop the work of the painter
      just
  Where paint leaves off and life begins—
  Put ice into the lines o' the poet when he
  Cries 'Next Stanza Fire!'—inscribe all
      human
  Effort with artistry's lamenting curse—
  The Incomplete!"

But here was a life unstained.
"Which of you accuseth me of
sin?" He could ask his enemies
without fear that any of them could
make such accusation. One who
saw him in that hour declared, "I
find no fault in him." A modern
teacher has called our attention to
the fact that here was a Baby born

44

in a cattle shed, brought up in a carpenter's home, working at the household trade until he was a full-grown man, then teaching his people for a few months until he died at the age of thirty-three years; who raised no armies, organized no institution, wrote no books, held no office; who was poor and unbefriended; called crazy by his family, called a heretic by his church, called a traitor by his nation, and finally dragged outside the walls of the city he loved and crucified as a felon between thieves. And yet after two thousand years there is not a land on earth where men and women would not gladly lay down their lives for the privilege of telling people about him. Do we not feel the wonder and splendor of such a life? Yet some use his name

only in profanity and some claim
to have no time for his service.
Rather before the splendor of such
unsullied character we should join
with Sidney Lanier,

"But Thee, O Sovereign Son of Time,
  But Thee, O Poet's Poet, Wisdom's Tongue,
  But Thee, O Man's best Man, O Love's
      best Love,
  Oh perfect life in perfect labor writ.
  Oh all men's Comrade, Servant, King and
      Priest
  What if or yet, what mote, what flaw, what
      lapse—
  What least defect or shadow of defect
  What rumor tattled by an enemy
  Of inference loose, what lack of grace
  Even in torture's grasp, or sleep's or
      death's—
  Oh what amiss may I forgive in Thee
  Jesus, Good Paragon, Thou Crystal
      Christ?"[1]

[1] From "The Crystal." Used by permission of Charles
Scribner's Sons, Publishers, New York.

46

2. The exhibition of what sin can do.

Looking at this picture we are reminded of another verse of Scripture, "And this is the condemnation, that light is come into the world, and men loved darkness rather than light, because their deeds were evil." Here we see what malice and perfidy have accomplished. The old law of retaliation was cruel—an eye for an eye, a tooth for a tooth, and a life for a life—but earth holds no cruelty so great as to compel the innocent to suffer for the guilty. In this picture we see the extreme expression of it.

It were well to look within our hearts to see if injustice and malice abide there. There are some who seem greatly disturbed lest science shall establish some connection be-

tween them and a simian ancestry.
Far more disturbing should be other
evidences of our brutish origin.
Some people have a tiger in them
and some have the disposition of a
snake. When we see the evidences
of our barbaric inheritance, our jun-
gle impulse but poorly concealed,
when we behold those who answer
the call of the wild or when we
hear that call ourselves, it but
proclaims man's need of salvation.
The subjugation of evil in our
own lives can be accomplished only
through a right relation with God.
Sin is an attitude. If the greatest commandment is to love God
with all the soul, heart, and mind,
then the greatest sin is the failure
to love God. "He that believeth
not is condemned already," and
as we look at this picture we see

what the unbelieving heart has done.

3. The exposition of divine love.

Here is the visual expression in color of that great utterance, "For God so loved the world, that he gave his only begotten Son, that whosoever believeth in him should not perish, but have everlasting life." If these mute lips could speak they might say,

"I gave, I gave my life for thee.
What hast thou given for me?"

4 An example of true discipleship.

Jesus said, "I have called you friends." Discipleship is friendship. Some think of it as theology, membership in a church, receiving a sacrament. The whole question of the Christian life would be greatly simplified if we could think of it in terms of friendship with Jesus.

49

Our friends are tested in trouble.
Then we learn who our true friends
are. Some of Jesus' friends forsook
him and fled, but there were others
who came forth and stood by his
side in that hour. There is nothing
in the world as beautiful as friendship like this. It is friendship of
this type which Raphael has portrayed upon the canvas of this picture. Here are Mary, the Mother,
with a broken heart, and Mary
Magdalene with gratitude unutterable. Here is Joseph of Arimathæa,
who offered his tomb as the resting
place of the Great Teacher. And
Nicodemus, a member of the Sanhe-
drin, who had believed but not
openly for fear of the Jews. They
were men of wealth and power.
At last they came forth and declared themselves. Faith conquered

fear. They gave testimony to the world of the love which they bore him.

Do you admire the teachings of Jesus and honor him because of his spotless life or his place in history? Come out of your hiding place and say so. Give him the advantage of your open declaration. Take your position courageously. Do not wait until others have done their worst to destroy and made their escape into the darkness. Come now, and be among those who are counted and counted on as belonging to Christ.

THE LAST SUPPER

To break bread together, from time immemorial has had something sacramental about it. The very invitation to dine is an offer of intimacy, a sign of friendship, a proof of confidence. When it is a parting meal a wistful sorrow pervades the occasion and the hour passes into memory as a treasured experience. When Jesus and his disciples ate their last supper in the upper room the simple procedure became a ceremony, and ever since it has been preserved in remembrance of him because there was something in it typical of his suffering and sacrifice.

On the walls of the Dominican Refectory at Milan one may see

THE LAST SUPPER

Da Vinci

THE LAST SUPPER

Da Vinci's great picture "The Last Supper." It is one of the world's masterpieces. In it there are beauty and majesty. The artist has not merely mixed pigments and spread colors, but has portrayed a spiritual message. The faces of the disciples delineate love, terror, anger, grief, bewilderment. Judas assumes the air of bravado. Jesus' countenance is a combination of strength and beauty. It is as though the picture were taken by snapshot, by that sudden photographic power which has preserved their expression in that tense moment when the Master said, "One of you shall betray me."

It required years to complete this picture. The Prior complained at the delay. William Wetmore Story has told in poetic form of this complaint and the artist's reply:

PICTURES THAT PREACH

"A picture is not wrought
  By hands alone, good Padre, but by
    thought.
  In the interior life it first must start
  And grow to form and color in the soul."

The period of time involved in the painting is also explained by the fact that the artist used human models and sometimes these were hard to find. We are told that Da Vinci found a young man in the choir of a cathedral, with a face so pure and spiritual, so mystical and divine that he used him as the model for Saint John. Years passed and the picture was nearly completed. He needed a model for Judas. He searched felons' cells and criminal resorts. There he found one whose face was the personification of evil. Ere it was copied into the picture he discovered that it was the same man who at an earlier time had posed as Saint John. His change of countenance from holiness to hideousness had been wrought by a life of sin.

In the picture Jesus sits singularly alone and on his face is an infinite sadness. Perhaps this is accounted for not by the fact that one is a traitor, but that all are weak. He knows that in the garden he will pray alone, that in the judgment hall there will be no sympathetic face, that in trouble he will be deserted and denied.

We are told that the artist has likewise given us an interpretation of a later development in the apostolic group. There is a portrayal of the various functions in the ministry. "He gave some, apostles; and some, prophets; and some, evangelists;

and some, pastors and teachers; . . . for the work of the ministry, for the edifying of the body of Christ." These are apparent in the four sub-groupings of the painting Beginning at the left, the evangelists are Andrew, James the less, and Nathanael; in the next group the apostles are Peter, and Judas, whose vacancy in the apostolic group was later filled by Matthias, and John. The teachers are James and Thomas and Philip; and the administrators are Matthew, Thaddeus, and Simon. It is not that their function can be exactly outlined. They are only suggested. Under the commission to carry the Master's message to the world, all such distinctions meet and merge.

What lessons are profitable for us?

1. There is room for all kinds of

people among the disciples of Jesus. Even more important than any ecc esiastical distinction which this apostolic company obtained through the assignment of any special duties is the more significant fact that they represented the differences and diversity of human nature Had we selected the disciples of Christ, we might have gone to some university, or to government officials, or to those who were successful in the market place. Jesus selected common people. What discouraging material it seems to be at times! There is scarcely one in the company that Jesus did not need to reprove. They were tardy of faith and obtuse of understanding. Studying them, one feels that the way of discipleship is open to all.

"I am not good enough" is oft-times used by people whose enlistment in church service is solicited. No one is good enough. Jesus has never had a perfect church. In one of Paul's letters he said, "I am the least of the apostles"; at a later date he wrote, that he was "less than the least of all saints," and at a still later date he declared that he was "the chief of sinners." As he grew in saintliness he grew in sensitiveness to sin. The persistency and place and power of Christianity in spite of the imperfections of its advocates is one of the proofs of its divine character. "The church is not a company of perfected saints, but of confessed sinners," said a great teacher. This is a unique distinction. Many others boast of their virtues. Candidates for office, applicants for positions, the principals in some sporting event, the man on the street does not hesitate at all to speak in terms of self-assurance and self-praise. Christians do not boast of their achievements—they con ess their need.

This is the primary qualification for discipleship:

> "All the fitness he requires
> Is to feel the need of him."

None are unwelcome. None need hesitate. Jesus is saying, "I have chosen you." Christ's table is an extension table and there is a place for everyone.

2. We are all called to the fellowship of his last days. "Can ye drink my cup?" the Master asks. To find the answer to that question is the problem of many. At the time of the Men and Religion Move-

ment in the city of Des Moines, when Raymond Robins was introduced, reference was made by the chairman to his religious experience in these terms: "He went into Alaska in search of the Golden Fleece and while there found the Holy Grail." When we are sinners we can be saved only by our dependence upon Christ; after we are Christians we can be saved only by accepting the dependence which he places upon us. We feel this commission in the atmosphere of this Last Supper.

It was Thursday night of Passion Week. In an upper room the disciples were gathered with their Master. Words had been spoken and counsel given that filled these men with a strange sense of responsibility. Outside, the city was asleep save for the footfall of an occasional passer-by upon the pavements below, save for the "All's well" of the watchman at the gates and walls, save for the malignant plotting of those in authority who were eager to apprehend this teacher from the hills of Galilee. The supper had been a sacrament. Every occasion may be a sacrament when Christ is present and his blessing is given. In the midst of it, Christ took up a cup and, lifting it with steady hand, spake, "This is my blood of the new testament which is shed for many." We have greatly used the Cross as a symbol of Christ's passion and suffering. He said, "Take up the cross, and follow me," but he also said, "Can ye drink of the cup that I drink of?" Thus the cup as well as the cross typifies his suffering.

It is not surprising that the early

church was quick to seize upon the cup and cross as symbols of Christianity. It is not more surprising that through the centuries traditions should have grown up about each. Wagner has gathered up some of these legends in his "Parsifal." Tennyson has done the same in his "Idyls of the King." Lowell in his "Vision of Sir Launfal" has expressed the social obligation of the gospel and has shown how the Holy Grail can be found only in service.

We may be glad that the cross of Christ and the cup of Christ have been lost. All the material side of his ministry has perished. There is something barbaric in all of us, and to have a shrine of sacred relics would only conduce to idol worship and defeat the spiritual purpose of the gospel. It was the deeper meaning that Christ had in mind when he asked, "Can ye drink of my cup?" He was not thinking merely of putting human lips to the rim of it. What he had in mind was their power of endurance their participation in suffering and their power to share with him in the redemption of the world. When they answered, "We are able," we are not sure that they fully understood.

We may not understand the mystery of how his suffering acted as a penalty for broken laws or became a substitute for a punishment which man deserved; but we do know that his suffering was redemptive in its purpose, for progress for the reign of God in the affairs of men.

Is not this his meaning?—We must enter into the Holy of holies of sacrifice and suffering for others and

go into the garden with its burdens,
and climb the hill with its cross,
that others may know the quality
and appeal of this divine love. We
must drink of this cup of his pain
and loneliness and struggle in order
that we may also drink his cup of
peace and inspiration

We must catch the spirit of Elsie's
prayer in "The Golden Legend":

"If my feeble prayer can reach thee,
O my Saviour, I beseech thee
Even as thou hast died for me
    More sincerely—
Let me follow where thou leadest,
Let me bleeding as thou bleedest
Die, if dying I may give
Life to one who asks to live,
    And more nearly
Dying thus, resemble thee."

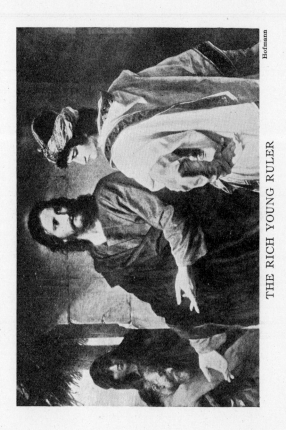

Hofmann

THE RICH YOUNG RULER

THE RICH YOUNG RULER

JESUS came to save humanity. No class cleavage or social strata kept him from the utmost friendship with all. Man-made distinctions meant nothing to him. There are those to-day who would make Jesus the exclusive servant of the lowly and the champion of economic readjustment, the opponent of wealth, and the friend of the poor. But this does not tell the whole story. "The common people heard him gladly," but also of "the chief rulers many believed on him." Garments coarse and homespun as well as robes of finest texture mingled in the crowds which followed him. He ate with publicans and sinners,

but likewise he was a guest at
Simon's banquet table. A nameless
Syrophœnician woman besought him
for her daughter, but, in a similar
fashion, a haughty Roman centurion
sought him for his son Peter, the
fisherman, said, "Thou art the
Christ," while a member of the San-
hedrin, Nicodemus by name, said,
"Thou art a teacher sent from God."
Blind beggars piteously cried after
him, but such was his ministry that
Joseph of Arimathæa, a man of
wealth, provided his tomb.

The peculiar interest in this incident of Jesus' ministry is in the
fact that he is dealing with a rich
young ruler. Think of the chance
the young man had. He was so
near the Kingdom and yet so far.

When Samuel Hadley, the superin-
tendent of the Water Street Mission,

was dying and realized that he was soon to leave his work, he cried out, piteously, "Who will take care of my poor bums now?" It was a beautiful expression of evangelistic passion which seeks the lowliest and the lost. An equal passion is needed to win college students with their powers of leadership in life's to-morrow. Who is crying out to-day with heart hunger for the salvation of business and professional men? Those who are rich in this world's goods and this world's honors are as much in need of the friendship of Christ as any prodigal in the far country. They seem so self-sufficient. They have everything. Often within their hearts there is loneliness unutterable because no one seems to care for their souls.

Let us look for a time at the

qualities of this young man. He had wealth and the confidence which it brings. There was personal charm also and when Jesus looked on him he loved him. By virtue of being a ruler we know that he was in a position of influence. The eyes of many were upon him and what he did was sure to receive the admiration of many. The fine quality of enthusiasm was in his life. He came "running." He went away "sad." Here are elation and depression—the extremes of emotion. What a trait this is! We are drawn inevitably to those who are capable of deep feeling. This is the peculiar possession of youth and gives us added appreciation for the rich young ruler. He came likewise with an open mind. "What shall I do that I may inherit eternal life?" It was

72

a natural question, for the Pharisees had always emphasized the necessity of "works." Candor is ever necessary to the discovery of truth. Let us place morality likewise to his credit. He could say concerning the commandments, "All these have I kept from my youth." What a recommendation! He was evidently in sympathy with religion and, so far as we know, was orthodox in his beliefs—a person of importance with attractive qualities and great possibilities. What an addition to the disciples of Christ! What an advantage if he might join this inner circle! What a chance to capitalize wealth and influence for a great cause! What an opportunity to strengthen the kingdom! Yet— "one thing thou lackest"; and because he made a great refusal instead of a great decision he goes away sorrowful, nameless, and doomed to oblivion.

Hofmann's picture portrays this dramatic moment. Study the contrast between these two young men! One with the rich garments of his station, the other in the seamless robe of his perfect life. One whose wealth was without, the other having wealth within. One expressing the genius of his life in the word "have," the other with the word "give." One standing with eyes averted and arms akimbo and fingers in-turned with grasping greed, the other with open countenance and outstretched arms and extended palms of generosity.

1. Consider the price of discipleship—"One thing thou lackest." One defect mars. Nothing is unim-

portant. It is not an unreasonable demand that Jesus makes. One torpedo sinks a ship. One broken rail wrecks a train. One severed wire breaks the connection between cities. One fatal shot from a schoolboy's revolver and a world is plunged into war.

"There is one black spot in every man's sunshine—the shadow of himself," said Thomas Carlyle. But it is possible for us to put this shadow behind us or beneath our feet. Jesus seeks this readjustment in human life. He makes a sharp issue between selfishness and service. He does not obscure the contrast between the world and Christianity. He challenges the strong, the confident, the resourceful. The genius of the gospel is not the erasure of social differences by legislative enact-

ments, but the lifting of the lowly
to higher levels by those whose lives
have been touched by the spirit of
Christ. "We then that are strong
ought to bear the infirmities of the
weak."

The world is full of unfortunate
and troubled people. Only the
strong can help. This spirit is
necessary to discipleship

2. Consider also the price of perfection. "If thou wilt be perfect,
go and sell that thou hast, and give
to the poor, and thou shalt have
treasure in heaven; and come and
follow me." Jesus laid his hand
upon the defect of his inner life.
Evidently it was not his riches but
his attitude toward his riches that
needed correction. He did not
charge him with selfishness. There
is always a last step, a final decision,

a full surrender. Jesus exemplifies this in his own experience and says to us, "Come and follow me."

Bishop Edwin H. Hughes tells of a prayer meeting which was held in a church upon the Pacific Coast, in which the question for discussion was, "If you had the choice of being some Bible character which one would you prefer to be?" An informal discussion of this interesting proposal was made. There were those who selected Abraham and Moses and some of the prophets. There were those who preferred the privilege of association with Christ and New-Testament history. In the group was a man who was the greatest of them all when measured by the ordinary standards of success, and ere the meeting closed he arose and said, very quietly, "As I look into my own heart to-night, I believe that of all those who are to be found in the Bible, I should rather be Simon of Cyrene that I might carry the cross of Christ for a little way."

" 'Take up thy cross,' the Saviour said,
  'If thou would'st my disciple be;
Deny thyself, the world forsake,
  And humbly follow after me.' "

"THE LIGHT OF THE WORLD" ^{Hunt}

"THE LIGHT OF THE WORLD"

"O Jesus, thou art standing
    Outside the fast-closed door;
In lowly patience waiting
    To pass the threshold o'er:
Shame on us, Christian brethren,
    His name and sign who bear:
Oh shame, thrice shame upon us,
    To keep him standing there!"

"BEHOLD I stand at the door, and knock: If any man hear my voice, and open the door, I will come in to him, and will sup with him, and he with me."

This is the scripture which is visualized in Holman Hunt's great masterpiece, "The Light of the World," which hangs upon the walls of the chapel of Keble College, Oxford. It is a marvelous picture done with exquisite coloring and minute attention to detail. Even

the facets of the jewels are clearly
marked and luminous with light.
The veins upon the leaves are visible. There is a mystery of color
and a blending of light and shade
that moves the soul to devotion and
worship. It is an evangelistic appeal
in color. It portrays the moment
when human destiny hangs in the
balance, when Divine Love patiently
waits upon human reluctance. Here
we see the perpetual issue between
heaven and earth. Here is the continual challenge from Christ to men.
Here we witness the ever-present
appeal of love to lethargy. It is a
call to decision done in oil and color.

On this canvas is portrayed the
door of the human soul—barred,
with nails and hinges rusty. It is
knitted and bound to the stanchions
by creeping ivy. A bat, the creature

of the night, hovers near. The threshold is overgrown with brambles and wild grass. Jesus approaches in the nighttime. He is garbed as prophet, priest, and king. The white robe denotes his prophetic office, the breastplate his priesthood, the crown of gold intertwined with thorns proclaims his royalty. He brings a twofold light. The lantern in his hand represents the light of conscience. It reveals sin. Its fire is red and fierce. Within its radiance fall the door, the weeds, an apple—symbol of man's first sin. The other light is from his face. It proclaims the hope of salvation. It is an illumination both subdued and sublime. His expression is as appealing as the tenderness of God.

So He stands at the door of each man's heart asking admittance.

1. What will happen if we do not open the door?

It will be our loss. Closing the door against him means to close it against the finest things in life. It means isolation and darkness. It proclaims our selfishness. It prophesies that some day we shall be left alone.

Suppose that you did not answer the knock at the door of your house. Think what you might miss. Perhaps someone came bearing a gift, someone with a message of cheer, someone offering friendship. How proud we are when some man of affairs—some person of distinction calls at our door! How gladly we open it to him! How honored we are by his recognition! With what enthusiasm we relate the incident! Have you ever thought that when Jesus knocks at the doors of our hearts it is a distinction far beyond that of earth? If we do not open to him who says, "I am come that they might have life, and that they might have it more abundantly," we suffer irreparable loss.

Furthermore, he will be disappointed. There is no latch or latch-string on the outside of this door. There is no way to secure admittance from the outside. The artist knew that in portraying the door of the human soul he dealt with a portal which can be opened only from within. Jesus will not force an entrance. He knocks, but will not batter down the door. He is a gentleman. He waits our willing welcome. He came all the way from heaven to earth to make this call, but has no expectation of coming in unless the door is opened from the inside. With what pathos we hear him say, "Ye will not come to me, that ye might have life." This is the perpetual heartbreak of Christ, that he should be again and again despised and rejected of men.

2. What will happen if we do open the door?

If we let him in, it were well to decide at once that he may come clear in. If we extend the courtesy of permitting him to pass the threshold, we must extend the further courtesy of making him feel at home. It is not satisfactory to permit him entrance into only one of the rooms of our life. It does not minister to peace to acknowledge that there are some rooms that would occasion embarrassment if he should look into them. We can hardly say, "Come in, but stay in the parlor." If anywhere about the place there are dirty linen and garbage cans and skeletons, we had better clear them out before he enters. If we have some friends in another room we would not like to have him meet, they had better be shown the door marked "Exit." He has a way with him and will want to set the house in order.

Once Jesus dined with Zacchæus, and something wonderful came into the life of the publican as the result of that visit. His whole attitude toward life and property changed because Jesus came into his house. He sat at Simon's banquet table, but ere the meal was ended such words were spoken to Simon as he had never heard before. He was welcomed into the home of Lazarus and Mary and Martha, and they yielded him their love. Even the good man of the house who furnished him an upper room discovered that shortly his guest had become host, the supper a sacrament, and the room the birthplace of the Christian Church.

So to-day when he enters into human life something wonderful appears. He has power to sanctify each room, to beautify each activity, to glorify each duty, and even as at Cana of old, turn the water of commonplace experiences into the wine of spiritual enjoyment.

"There's a Stranger at the door,
    Let him in;
He has been there oft before,
    Let him in.
Let him in, ere he is gone,
Let him in, the Holy One.
Jesus Christ, the Father's Son,
    Let him in."

BREAKING THE HOME TIES

At the Columbian Exposition in Chicago, in 1893 Thomas Hovenden's great picture "Breaking the Home Ties" first came to public notice. It was one of the sensations of that summer. Crowds were arrested in their pursuit of pleasure, in their quest of things new and curious and wonderful, by the tender appeal of its message. The room where the canvas hung was always crowded. Faces were wet with tears. People came back again and again for its message. The story of visitors to the World's Fair was sure to include a recital of the interest and influence this picture had on the moving multitude. It secured a popularity at that time which has persisted through the years. Its emotional appeal is gripping. It visualizes an incident that occurs in family life throughout the world. It is not surprising that it has found its way into the Young Men's Christian Association buildings throughout the land.

A country boy is leaving home for the city. The father is already on his way to the door with the luggage, thus turning his face away from the tender farewell of the boy's mother, and so hiding the emotion we know he keenly feels. Grandmother sits at the table dreaming of other days. Little sister does not know the meaning of it all, but her face is sad at the parting of her big brother. The collie is aquiver with excitement, feeling this event is ominous. The mother looks lovingly into the lad's eyes, her hands are on his shoulders, anxiety is written on her face, in her heart she is praying and hoping. "Will he come back again as clean and noble as in this hour?" she wonders. Here is a love that cannot let him go and yet she knows it impossible to keep him forever at the fireside. The boy looks into space. For the moment he sees not the humble surroundings of his home, the breakfast table from which the family has just arisen, the rag carpet, the cupboard, the mantle with its candelabra, the incidental items that make up the furn'shing of his home and shall later be recalled as memory weaves its charm upon his lonely heart. He sees not even the sweet face of his dear mother. He sees the castle of dreams. He catches sight of the city with its glitter and glamour. He sees the beckoning hands that invite his soul to go forth in the great adventure.

Oh, holy hour when youth sets forth to make conquest of the world! There comes a time when life must be measured in achievement. The urge of something within demands that we try our powers on the wait-ing world. The youth feels a sense of independence. The fledgling's wings grow strong enough to venture in the air. The young man and maiden leave home for college, for the city, for a career urged on by ambition, but ever followed by loving hearts which pray for their safety and success.

"Is the young man safe?" cried David in tremulous anxiety as run-ners came to report a battle in which his own son was involved. The young man Absalom, with handsome appearance and ingratiating manner and keen wit, had turned his powers to base purposes and led an insurrection against his father. But his waywardness did not destroy his father's love. Nor does it to-day. The parent impulse is ever the same. "Is he safe?" How many homes there are where sleep would be sweet if parents could be sure, where songs would brighten the day if father and mother could in their hearts be certain their loved ones were secure. Who knows but that much of such anxiety is also a speculation as to whether the home did its best ere the ties were broken, a consideration of partial responsibility should failure or shame overtake the one they love?

Youth goes forth into a new environment and amid new associations. Temptations lurk in hidden and unsuspected places. The subtle suggestion to do in Rome as Romans do has power to break down restraints and reserves. It takes real conviction and courage to do right whether you are in Rome or your own home town. How can the safety of youth be guaranteed as it goes out to make its own decisions and be responsible for them when they are made?

There are two elements which greatly contribute to the safety of youth when home ties are broken— instincts and ideals. Both may be definitely contributed to his equipment by the home.

1. The instinct of danger often saves him in times of decision. We

see it in nature. It is said that rats will desert a sinking ship! Wild animals will come into the clearings and seek the protection of man when forest fires travel their red path. Before an earthquake animals exhibit a strange restlessness, and one who was in San Francisco at the time disaster befell that city, says that in passing a livery stable a little before the shock he heard hoofs beating a veritable tattoo.

The soul has been made sensitive to danger likewise. The impulse to wait and weigh a doubtful matter, the restraint felt in times of temptation, the fear of sin and its consequences are in part God's way of answering the prayer "Deliver us from evil."

Ocean ships are equipped with sensitive thermometers submerged

near the prow that detect the presence and proximity of icebergs by
a falling temperature of the water.
Thus they escape collision.

Is not this what is meant when
we sing?—

> "I want a principle within,
>   Of jealous, godly fear;
> A sensibility of sin,
>   A pain to feel it near:
> I want the first approach to feel
>   Of pride, or fond desire;
> To catch the wandering of my will,
>   And quench the kindling fire."

Youth, with its exuberant spirit,
its abounding vitality, its overplus
of energy, must know how to use
and master these forces which are
resident within. They need spiritual
direction. They will not go wrong
if all the instincts have been trained
and nourished through prayer and

devotion. This is one function of the home.

2. Proper ideals are also necessary to guide life aright. Youth wants a "good time." Youth is entitled to a good time. It is the place of the home to see that even such an ideal as this is valid and good times are possible in which there is no regret, no day after, no soiling of the soul with smut, no mortgaging of the future with sins which rob one of vitality.

In J. G. Holland's "Katrina" is a passage of rare beauty touching the ideals of youth. An incident of childhood furnishes hope to a mother's heart. A pet lamb runs away and the lad recovers him on a hilltop near by. Then the mother says,

"My Paul has climbed the noblest mountain height

In all his little world—and gazed on scenes
As beautiful as rest beneath the sun.
I trust he will remember all his life
That to his best achievement, and the spot
Nearest to heaven his youthful feet have
    trod
He has been guided by a guileless lamb!
It is an omen which his mother's heart
Will cherish with her jewels."[1]

Happy the youth whose ideals are shaped by the Lamb of God. Jesus has power to lead youth to the heights of real achievement. If the home has done its duty, then when the children go out into the world for themselves they will find that the ties are not broken at all, but strengthened through separation into an appreciation that grows through the years.

---

[1] Used by permission of Charles Scribner's Sons, publishers, New York.

"HOPE"

Watts

"HOPE"

"My intention has not been so much to paint a picture that will charm the eye as to suggest thoughts that will appeal to the imagination and heart and kindle all that is best and noble in humanity."

Such is the statement of George Frederick Watts. As an artist he felt a call to service, a sense of a real mission to be fulfilled, a consciousness of divine appointment to his task. The spirit of his work is reflected in his picture, "Hope." Some critics have thought him a gloomy pessimist. Here is a picture of one who is apparently in despair. The eyes of the stooping figure are bandaged because if the facts were faced, hope would cease. The text Watts had in mind when he made this picture was, "We are saved by hope. But hope that is seen is not hope, for what a man seeth why doth he yet hope for?" The artist's purpose was to portray a vital and valid emotion in human experience.

Let us see in the picture rather the soul surmounting the world, a star in the sky, listening to a single note when all the strings on the harp of life have been broken but one—hope! Would that this vibrating string with its subtle harmony might ever sing its way into the soul! Meet life with a harp! Make life a melodious thing! Keep in tune! He who can strike a few harmonious notes into every situation is a benefactor indeed. The music-maker has a mission. Everyone who

can sing with hope when misfortune,
disaster, and death have done their
worst, may expect that the world
will stop and listen.

The harp is one of the world's
oldest musical instruments. It appears in mural paintings in The-
ban tombs. David was its master.
Homer is delineated in Greek sculp-
ture with a harp in his hand.
Painters of the Renaissance used it
freely. We have always thought of
it as one of the instruments used by
the heavenly hosts.

> "Angel voices, ever singing,
>   Round thy throne of light,
> Angel harps forever ringing,
>   Rest not day or night;
> Thousands only live to bless thee,
>   And confess thee Lord of might."

In the National Museum at Dublin
is to be seen one of the oldest relics

of Ireland—the harp of King Brian
Boru. In early Irish history harpers
went from place to place stirring the
people to patriotism. The harper
was associated with the king as
councilor. The harp was an emblem
upon the Irish flag for centuries.
They have ever been a people of
sentiment, poetry, and song. It is
different now. Even Tom Moore
told us of the change—

"The harp that once in Tara's halls
   The soul of music shed
Now hangs as mute on Tara's walls
   As if that soul were fled.
No more to chiefs and ladies bright
   The harp on Tara swells;
The chord alone that breaks the night
   Its tale of ruin tells."

How much more is this true to-day!
It would seem the soul of Ireland
has fled—the spirit of poesy crushed

by revolution and religious warfare
—a lovely land ruined by the smudge
of smoke and stain of blood.

A few miles from Paris is Mal
Maisson, the summer home of Napo-
leon and Josephine. In the music
room one may see a harp with
broken strings. There is something
pathetic in its appearance. It would
seem to stand for the harp of love
broken not by time, but by faith-
lessness.

But the world cannot be saved by
the music from the harp of patriotism, however stirring its strains or
played with whatever impetuous zeal
or nimble fingers. Nor can it be
saved by the music from the harp
of love, however appealing and tender its note. The music of religious
faith and hope is needed. In Watts'
picture the planet whirls in space

amid skies overcast with clouds, and when the strings of every experience and emotion on the harp of life have been broken save one, the soul leans and listens to the message sweet and low that comes from the throbbing string of hope.

The Bible is a book of hope. It approves and praises this resilient quality of life which comes back from every trouble with a rebound. "Now, Lord, what wait I for? My hope is in thee." Every prophet is a messenger of hope. However foreboding the spiritual destitution of his times, he ever closed his message —"Better times coming." Jesus was an apostle of good cheer. He greeted those in trouble with this salutation. He bade his followers be of good cheer in the face of disaster and death. The early church preached a gospel of hope. "We are saved by hope." Someone has said that faith is salvation looking up, grace is salvation looking beneath, love is salvation looking around, hope is salvation looking beyond.

Paul once said, "If in this life only we have hope, we would be of all men most miserable." But hope always helps here and now. Life is given buoyancy by it. Like fishermen's nets, the sorrows of life bear us down as with leaden weights, but hope gives buoyancy and saves us for usefulness.

Christian hope is something more than Watts has portrayed. Watts' picture is one of hope against hope. Christian hope takes the bandages from the eyes and makes it possible for us to see the star through a rift in the clouds. Christian hope does not go with head down, but with face upturned and radiant. Christian hope does not believe the planet is lost in a maze of clouds, but, rather, that "the whole world rolls into light, it is daybreak everywhere." Christian hope is not content to touch the one remaining string and listen to its solitary note, but restrings the harp of life and sweeps them all once more into melody.

"Love took up the harp of life,
Smote on all its chords with might,
Smote the chord of self which, trembling,
Passed in music, out of sight."

CHRIST IN GETHSEMANE

Hofmann

CHRIST IN GETHSEMANE

"HE went a little further, and fell on his face, and prayed, saying, O my Father, if it be possible, let this cup pass from me: nevertheless, not as I will, but as thou wilt." That which Matthew set forth in words Hofmann has set forth in paint and canvas. Before such a scene one is silent. The soul is hushed in the presence of this cry of suffering. A mystery we cannot understand and before which we dare not be too curious broods over this night scene. Those who have been called to enter some Garden of Gethsemane and there have fallen under some crushing weight of woe find a fellowship in this picture others cannot appreciate. Let us withdraw into the shadows and consider its meaning. Let us meditate not upon its message to the sorrowing, but to service.

Back of every supreme achievement is a supreme endeavor.

Great things do not happen. A submarine cable is not an accident. A transcontinental train is not a creation of the magician's wand. A daily paper with the imprint of world events upon it does not issue from the flying presses at the snap of the editor's fingers. Back of all the marvelous devices of our civilization are the organizing genius and energy of man.

No one wins success in any field easily. Success is a shy maiden whose smiles are won only by ardent wooers; a pearl lying in dark depths

where only the diver who is willing
to risk his life in the plunge may
hope to find it; a ledge of gold along
a mountain side where only the
hardy miner stalwart of limb may
climb; a prize at the goal which
only the swiftest, fleetest runner in
life's race may hope to seize.

Great achievements are wrought
by those who have the capacity, the
patience, the courage, to go a "little
further" than anyone else has ven-
tured.

Audubon, the naturalist and orni-
thologist, whose name is inseparably
associated with the creatures of the
sky, who knew the song of the spar-
row and the nightingale, who saw
the eagle leap from his eerie and
circle into the blue, as well as the
wren twittering at his eaves, made
as a result of his investigations a

great many original drawings. He went into the woods for several months, leaving them in a wooden box in the care of a friend. Returning, he found that two rats had made their home in the box. His beautiful drawings of a thousand creatures of the air were gnawed to bits. Thus the effort of a lifetime was destroyed. It almost unbalanced his mind. "But after a few days," he says, "I took up my gun, my note book, my pencil, and went back to the woods as gayly as if nothing had happened and by three years I had filled my folio again."

One of the finest pieces of writing that ever came from the hand of Thomas Carlyle was his interpretation of the French Revolution. He loaned the manuscript of the first volume to a friend, and when he asked for its return, it was discovered that the servant, seeing upon her master's desk what she thought was wastepaper, had used it to start a fire. But Carlyle did not despair. It is not recorded what he said. Let us not inquire. He rewrote the book from memory.

Thomas Edison, who holds the patents for a thousand inventions, had difficulty in perfecting the phonograph. The reproduction of the human voice was perfect except for the sibilant. He could not make his machine sound the "s." He would say "specia" and the machine would say "pecia." It defied him. But settling himself to the task he labored for seven months incessantly —seventeen and eighteen hours each day—and then he triumphed.

One of the finest poems catching

up the spirit of conquest and breath-
ing patriotism is the poem by
Joaquin Miller, "Columbus." You
cannot forget it. Its lines draw a
picture of the fearful crew and the
stout-hearted man who issued the
orders despite tempest, despite uncer-
tainty, despite mutiny, "Sail on,
sail on." And when the mate and
his mutinous comrades would have
turned back, the Admiral was willing to go a little further.

"Then pale and worn, he kept his deck
    And peered through darkness. Ah, that
        night
Of all dark nights! And then a speck—
    A light! a light! a light! a light:
It grew, a star-lit flag unfurled!
    It grew to be Time's burst of dawn.
He gained the world; he gave that world
    Its grandest lesson—'On, sail on!' "[1]

---

[1] Permission to use poem "Columbus" rented to Harr
Wagner Publishing Company, Publishers of Joaquin Miller's
Complete Poems.

CHRIST IN GETHSEMANE

It is this disposition to go "a little further" that lifts all endeavor and achievement above the plane of mediocrity, that rescues it from the commonplace, that gives it the stamp of genius, that rewards it with the applause of men, that exalts it where a world gazes and wonders.

It is the ability to go a little further that makes an artist of the painter, tracing lines of loveliness on canvas which becomes immortal. It makes an orator of the public speaker, compelling and captivating and convincing those who hear. It makes a statesman of a politician with centuries and continents in his brain. It makes a poet of the rimester, catching the music of the spheres and the music of the fields and streams, and, best of all, the music of the human heart and weaving it into strains that lighten care and minister to happiness.

And here is our Divine Master rendering the supremest endeavor in the supremest realm and accomplishing a supreme achievement. Just as all toilers who have it in their hearts to render a surpassing service find themselves gradually separated from the multitude, so Christ in his desire to redeem the world leaves the crowds that throng him on every side, leaves the Temple area with its worshipers, leaves the city streets with its traffic and travelers, leaves the group that follows him with confidence, leaves the daylight where eyes peer and curiosity is awake—leaves all, that he may with a few take a path from the city gate, cross a brook, enter a garden where the silence broods and the stars keep vigil. Then, leaving a group of even his intimates, he goes forward where the three who knew him best are also left and he himself "went a little further"—falling on his face crushed with the world's woe, heart-broken for humanity's sin, alone, alone, crying out, "If it be possible—Not my will but thine be done!"

There had been many who had wrought works of righteousness for the world's redemption before Christ came. The vision of God's holiness and purity had flashed before one generation after another   Moses had seen his glory, and came from Sinai an interpreter of the moral law. Prophets again and again gave utterance to the high ideals of the spiritual kingdom.   Martyrs to the truth had died, seeing its triumph afar off.

But there was needed Someone who in this spiritual realm, this moral kingdom was able to go "a little further"—further than law-giver, than prophet, than martyr, than philosopher, than priest, than king. There was needed a Saviour who, in the supremest offering of himself, in a sacrifice unlike that which man could offer, would lift the standard of character to its highest pinnacle; One who being the brightness of God's glory, the express image of the Divine, nevertheless would stoop so low as to get his fingers under the bottom of the world's sin and misery and then lift the burden so high that it was placed penitent and believing at the feet of God.

CHRIST IN GETHSEMANE

The whole lesson in this incident is opulence of endeavor. Nowhere is there greater need for this than in Christian activity. So much effort in church life falls short of achievement. We grow weary of well doing.

Andrew Carnegie, in addressing a group of young men some years ago, said this significant thing bearing upon achievement, "Do your duty and a little more." You cannot cheat people out of success and promotion if that is their spirit. You cannot stop the progress of a church that is filled with people who are imbued with that spirit. It is the task we do when our heart sings that is well done. It is the consecration that is joyous that God honors. It is the labor that is spontaneous and glad-hearted that is most effective. If we mean it when

we say, "I love thy church, O God,"
then its services are a delight, its
worship a benediction, its interests
an inspiration, its tasks a pleasure.

There is a distinct relation we
are to maintain to that kneeling
Figure in the garden. Are we like
the city wrapped in slumber after
having given to the Master but a
momentary thought—indifferent to
where he is or what his fate may
be? Are we like those in authority
—intent on doing him injury, lay-
ing plans to overthrow him, check
his influence, defeat his message?
Are we among those who follow his
leadership, but with blundering faith,
with lack-luster interest, with un-
certain feeling about the outcome of
it all—and therefore left at the edge
of the garden because we cannot
sympathize or understand? Are we

among those most intimate and appreciative, but even while the Master prays, overcome with sleep, failing to watch and pray and enter into the fellowship of his sufferings?

Oh crowd close to the Master! Go a little further in your devotion to him. Get under the interests of his kingdom with all your resources —a little further in loyalty, a little further in prayer life, a little further in church attendance, a little further in soul-growth, a little further in generosity, a little further in cooperation, a little further in helping people, a little further in consecration and enthusiasm for the kingdom of God.

THE LOST SHEEP

KNOWLEDGE of Bible countries and custom greatly helps in the understanding of its message. Renan said that a trip through Palestine was a fifth Gospel. The traveler in the Holy Land soon discovers it to be a grazing country. He will hear the tinkle of the sheep bell. He will find flocks on the slopes of hills and in the valleys. The people are pastoral.

When Jesus used the figure of the sheep and the shepherd it was one of their everyday life, the language of a common industry which all understood.

The picture of "The Lost Sheep," by Soord, visualizes for us the par-

Soord

THE LOST SHEEP

able in which with a few skillful strokes Jesus himself painted a picture—"What man of you, having an hundred sheep, if he lose one of them, doth not leave the ninety and nine in the wilderness, and go after that which is lost, until he find it?" No commentary, no sermon, no homily could be as eloquent an exposition as this canvas. It is a description of Jesus' own ministry.

While the name of this picture is "The Lost Sheep," and has been called by some "The Ninety and Nine," one prefers to designate it as "The Good Shepherd." Artists very early in the Christian era used this symbol for the Christ. Through the centuries he has been delineated as the shepherd who carries the lambs in his arms, walks beside still waters, holds the staff in his hand, and leads the flock to plenteous pasture. It is ever a picture of the daylight. His countenance is always one of benignity and peace.

How different this picture of the Good Shepherd. It is a picture of the night. Canyon depths are still sleeping in the darkness and dawn is barely tipping the mountain's rim. Through the cavern has echoed the piteous cry of this helpless sheep. A vulture in wheeling flight waits his prey. Caught in the brambles upon a ledge of rock it is impossible to escape without help. Into this situation the good shepherd has come. Far over the precipice he leans in his work of rescue. We cannot see his face. In this picture it is not his portrait but his posture that reveals his character and his love.

THE LOST SHEEP

1. The picture proclaims the value of one. The whole flock was safe—only one lost sheep. How many were in the flock we do not care. The fact that one was lost gave tragic meaning to the value of one.

No man can say, "I do not count." None can say, "God does not care." This picture preaches Heaven's interest in the earth—God's outreach after man, a divine solicitude so personal and intimate that the recovered soul may ever say and sing, "He loved me and gave himself for me."

We often say that we cannot measure the growth of the Kingdom by statistics. Truly there is much good that cannot be tabulated in a year book. He who undertakes to catalogue and card index such a thing as character assumes too difficult a task.

But let us not overlook the regard which God has for numbers. There is a book in the Bible called Numbers. It may not prove very interesting reading from a devotional standpoint, but how wonderful it is to learn that God kept count of his people. Jesus did not talk in terms of groups. He had twelve disciples. He sent seventy forth with his message. He noted that there were ten lepers and that only one returned to give glory to God. When John and his associates went fishing he tells there were one hundred and fifty-three in the net and that they were big ones. God calls the stars by name, insignificant and numerous as they seem in the sky. "The very hairs of your head are numbered," we are told.

The glory of the gospel is indi-

vidual redemption which it provides.
The truest social salvation is accomplished by the transforming of single
souls. The most effective reform is
a revival. It were well to think in
terms of statistics in relation to the
kingdom of God and give more
anxiety to those who are out of the
fold rather than those who are
in it.

2. Responsibility brings rejoicing.
The keenest pleasures we have are
those not of ease but activity. To
coddle one's preferences, permit no
inconvenience to displace one's plans,
to never allow something that must
be done to interfere with meals or
sleep is to live a life of selfishness.
If the lost are ever saved, it will
be by those who are familiar with
the way. If the weak are ever
rescued, it will be by the strong

who have the power to love and
lift.

It is no special concern how this
sheep was lost. It probably never
intended to get lost. It went where
the sweet grass invited. It took a
wrong path. Then there was panic
and fear. In dealing with the lost
of earth there is no time for argu-
ments and explanations. It is no
time for a hireling. Some one is
missing, therefore let the alarm be
sounded. The task of recovery is
imperative and urgent.

What a thrill comes to the heart
when we feel that we have been
able to rescue another! Such an
event is celebrated in heaven. The
rapture we feel is perchance com-
municated to us from the skies.

3. Love that persists. There have
been some beautiful passages which

describe the Good Shepherd. "He giveth his life for the sheep"—"All we like sheep have gone astray"— stampeding toward ruin! Then God sent the Good Shepherd to straighten out the confusion, to quiet fears, to rescue the mission. "I know my sheep, and I am known of mine."

But there is nothing so wonderful about the Good Shepherd as this simple phrase "until he find it." That is the text for this picture. The shepherd cannot put his work upon an eight-hour schedule. He cannot think of safety first. There must be no counseling with comfort. There must be no fear of the night or the creatures in it. "Until he find it"—here is service that succeeds, rescue that turns to rejoicing, despair that changes to delight as the day breaks.

PICTURES THAT PREACH

The Master told of a shepherd true
  Who counted his sheep at the close of
    the day
And found one lost—so the whole night
    through
He sought till he found the one astray.
From out of the night and the storm he
    came
  To the safe corral, with a joy elate,
And calling the lost by its chosen name
  He placed it inside of the wicket gate.

'Tis a simple story he told them then,
  And a simple task that the shepherd had.
The Master a shepherd himself to men
  Gave proof of his love for the lost and
    bad.
But shepherds he sets o'er his flocks to-day
  Find their work complex and the journey
    long.
The lost are many and dawn is gray
  Ere their work is done with the human
    throng.

Not in the mountains they seek his sheep,
  But in lofty buildings of steel and stone,

THE LOST SHEEP

Where men must ponder their problems
    deep
    And fight the battle of life alone.
In offices high, keys constantly click
    And tell off the gain or the loss of the day,
And here, they know, there are hearts that
    are sick
    And some who have doubted, and lost
    the way.

Not in the desert that's wild and bare,
    With its burning heat and its wide
    expanse;
But the desert they find up the shaking
    stair
    Mid the tiny rooms where the shifting
    glance
Of the hunted souls who tremble and fear
    Lest hunger and sickness o'ertake their
    brood—
To these they give of their alms and cheer,
    And tell them of Christ, the Living Food.

Not in the shadows of night alone,
    Does the modern shepherd find those
    who need,

PICTURES THAT PREACH

But out in the street where the undertone
    Of the hurrying traffic, driven by greed,
Is mingled with voices of women and men
    With music from theater, hall, café;
Out there he searches again and again—
    Out in the city's Great White Way.

Not in the silence of solitude,
    Away from the marts and haunts of men,
Where the noise of the street finds interlude
    Of peaceful quiet in woods or glen;
But the modern shepherd now seeks the lost
    Where the human tides in their fullness
        sweep,
Where passion and strife like waves are
        tossed
    On the restless surface of life's vast deep.

Not for just one that is lost from the fold
    Does the pastor of peoples now pray and
        toil—
He feels the weight of a burden rolled
    On his anxious soul. 'Tis the heart's
        recoil
From the sins of the day with their subtle
        lure,

THE LOST SHEEP

'Tis the love that would save them which
    sends him forth
To the many—how many he cannot be
    sure—
    To the East and the West, to the South
    and the North.

The shepherd who sought for that one lost
    sheep
    Thought not of himself till the lost was
    found.
O Shepherd of shepherds, thy vigil keep
    In us thy shepherds the whole year
    round;
That everywhere in the world of men,
    In the stress of these complex, modern
    days,
We may serve as we wish that it might
    have been
    When at last we are done and await thy
    praise.

THE LAST JUDGMENT

THE famous painting by Michael Angelo covers one end of the Sistine Chapel in Rome. This famous artist, who obtained distinction as a poet, a sculptor, an architect, and a painter, consumed three years in the completion of this picture. None were allowed to see the work as it progressed. When at last it was unveiled to the public there was consternation and criticism. Michael Angelo took the message of Dante and translated it into fresco. Jesus, at the very center of the picture, is a young Jove in wrath, consigning souls to the torment of scorching flame and writhing serpents. He is assisted by apostles and angels who push back into the flames any who

try to escape their suffering. The
saints in heaven look upon the
sinners in hell with complacency
and satisfaction. Here mediæval
theology is turned into visible night-
mare.

There is a story that among those
who severely criticized this picture
of Michael Angelo was the papal
secretary. He carried his complaint
to the Pope himself The artist
hearing of the criticism, went back
to his canvas and painted the face
of the papal secretary into one of
the figures, giving him the ears of
an ass and putting a serpent around
his body. This infuriated the secretary, as might well be expected.
When he went once more to the
Pope regarding the matter it is
said that the Pope replied, "If
Michael Angelo had put you in

purgatory, I could have got you out, but he has put you in hell, and there you must stay."

In matters of human judgment how characteristic this is! We put into our pictures and our opinions our own personal prejudices.

The solemnity of eternity forever rests upon the thought of judgment. Men were prostrated under the preaching of Jonathan Edwards on "Sinners in the Hands of an Angry God." The measures of Milton's "Paradise Lost" are the judgment of God set to music. To-day God has been interpreted in terms of judgment. We are told this dispensation is about to end. There are those who apparently rejoice in a triumph of Jesus which shall bring humiliation and suffering to great numbers. They foretell with rapt elation of coming separations. They conceive Jesus doing by force what he has not been able to accomplish by the nobility of his example or the power of his cross.

Let us inquire, therefore, what is meant by the judgment of Jesus.

1. It is present. "Now is the judgment of this world ' ' He that believeth not is condemned already." "This is the condemnation, that light is come into the world, and men loved darkness rather than light, because their deeds were evil." We do not have to wait for a great assize. It is not necessary to ponder possible decrees that may determine destiny. You may read your own fate now by your attitude of soul.

We are not taught that there is any moral transformation in death. There is no alchemy by which bad

141

becomes good in such an hour. A man's death-day is not Judgment Day. Every day is Judgment Day.

When death shall come we cannot know. Carlyle, picturing the death of Louis XV, said: "Death hath found thee—No palace walls or life guards or gorgeous tapestries or gilt buckram or stiffest ceremonial could keep him out. But he is here, and at thy very life breath, and will extinguish it." That hour comes to everyone.

A traveling man confided a few of his opinions to his seat companion on a railway train who chanced to be a preacher. Evidently, business had been poor that day—perhaps it had been poor for many days to develop the grouch he had.

"Every avenue leads to hell," he

declared: "Every avenue leads to hell. When I go to church I hear a narrow preacher. I hear discords in the choir. I get a hypocritical welcome and sit for an hour in a room that has not been ventilated for a week. It is the same everywhere. Business is rotten." "My dear fellow," said the preacher, mildly, "you don't need to worry about every avenue leading to hell —you're in hell now."

A darky of the old school was asked concerning the doctrine of election and he replied: "Election? Why, it's dis a way; God's votin' fo' yo, and de debbil is votin' agin yo'—and the election goes whichever way yo' votes yer own self."

We are voting to-day by our thoughts, speech, actions, moods. "Now is the judgment of this world." "The mind itself can make a heaven of hell and a hell of heaven." Paul in the Mamartine prison was able to dwell in heavenly places in Christ Jesus. A good saint once sang:

"Thy presence makes my paradise
And where thou art is heaven."

2. It is a process. "Now shall the prince of this world be cast out." The verb passes from the present to the future. Judgment is not an event but an eventuality. The process is in operation and comes at last to its climax. Final judgment is an extension of present judgment. We have a distinct relation to two worlds. We believe our consciousness shall be the same in each. We believe that the moral distinctions of both are the same. Our destiny is fixed not by an

arbitrary decree and is not the result of caprice. "Come, ye blessed," and "Depart, ye cursed," do not represent the fiat of a dictator, but are the inevitable culmination of our own conduct and rest upon distinctions which we are making here and now: "Inasmuch as ye did it," or "Inasmuch as ye did it not."

We can see this process at work all around us. There is something revelatory in both sin and righteousness. Jesus said, "There is nothing covered, that shall not . . . be known." If we live with sin, it will announce its presence. Jealousy twists the eyebrows. Cynicism curls the lips. Hatred distorts the smile. Covetousness hardens the face. The criminal comes to confession whether he would or not. Likewise when we pray in secret we are rewarded openly. Someone has said, "Prayers make the countenance their divinest altar." Edwin Markham has set this forth in a poem:

"Bishops and deans, would you detect
The crowning mark of the Elect—
Know who believe beyond rebuke
The Gospel and the Pentateuch—
Know who accept the Thirty-nine,
And taste with Christ the mystic wine?
Then search the face of him you doubt
And that will let the secret out.
Explore the face, and do not spare:
The Book of Life is written there!

"And would you know the other host,
Those that profane the Holy Ghost,
Those that deny the Ancient Word
The seers upon the mountain heard?
Then search the countenance, and trace
Their heresies upon the face:
That hardened line, that loveless look,
Are records in the Judgment Book.
The truth is written and writ plain
Whether we be for Christ or Cain.

"So shut the books about it all—
Shut Augustine, shut Ingersoll,
Aquinus, Calvin, tome by tome—
Shut Schleiermacher, shut Jerome.
Look on the face, for written there
The final judgments are laid bare.
The name is on the forehead writ
Of all that with the seraphs sit—
Of all that stumble toward the Pit."[1]

3. It is personal. By this is
meant the fact that the Judgment
of Jesus is a Judgment of personal
relationships. We judge by pre-
cepts and prohibitions. We go by
rules and regulations. We keep
books of law and have respect for
precedents. The Judgment of Jesus
would seem to involve more than
this. His Judgment takes into ac-
count the spirit of our lives. We
glibly specify who we think is right
or wrong. Asked to name the vil-

---

[1] Used by permission of author.

lain, we specify some crime. The villains, in Jesus' opinion, seemed to be those who did nothing—the priest and Levite who passed by on the other side, the rich man who allowed a beggar to go hungry at his gate, the servant who hid his talent in a napkin. Jesus takes personal offense at such neglect. Likewise he takes personal gratification in kindly and unselfish service which is rendered. Inasmuch as ye did it, or inasmuch as ye did it not unto one of the least of these, ye did it or ye did it not unto me.

THE ANGELUS

Millet

THE ANGELUS

"Far, far away,
  Like bells at evening pealing,
    The voice of Jesus sounds o'er land and
      sea;
  And laden souls by thousands meekly
    stealing,
    Kind Shepherd, turn their weary steps
      to thee."

"IT is the Angelus, the real thing;
I can hear the bell!" exclaimed the
artist François Millet when he completed this painting. He tried to
convey the devotional feeling of
peasants when at the close of day
they pause for prayer before returning home. It is a scene in rural
France. Devout souls rest from
work for purposes of devotion. It
is the prayer of the common people,
peasants in a potato field, prayer

amid toil, prayer in response to the call from the distant church tower. It is a picture full of beauty and inspiration. Viewing it one listens as well as looks. It puts sound on canvas.

Surely here is a picture that preaches. A message is proclaimed in unmistakable appeal to the soul. Shortly before it was painted Millet stood with his wife looking through a shop window at a picture that had recently been sold. Both were silent. Both felt alike. Presently the wife spoke—"That picture is not worthy of you."

"I know it," he replied, "but you know we needed the money." Again silence—then she pressed his arm.

"We can starve," she said, quietly, "but we can never paint a picture like that again."

THE ANGELUS

"The Angelus" was his next picture, and into it went the soul of the artist and the high resolve of that decisive hour. Certain ideals he cherished in his work were likewise attributable to his mother, who once said to him, "Remember you were a Christian before you were a painter." What good counsel! What transformation would be wrought if we held this important fact in constant remembrance!

The other day in a business office I saw a wall sign which read "Accuracy First." We have heard "America First" too long and too much. "Safety First" has led to the conservation of human life by protection from accidents, but all men understand that although self-preservation may be the first law of life it is by no means the highest law by which to live. Let us say, rather, "God First." "In the beginning God." We ask a blessing before the food we eat. Why not before a conversation, before reading a book, before going on a journey, before the work of a day? Benjamin Franklin once requested on the floor of the Constitutional Convention that the delegates engage in prayer for divine wisdom in the solution of some baffling problem over which days of debate had been spent. Has anyone heard of such a suggestion in Congress recently? Our times need the consciousness of God. It can come only through prayer.

1. "The Angelus" suggests family prayer. Back of this scene, yonder in the cluster of dwellings near the church, is a home. The artist has

done on canvas what Robert Burns did in verse when he wrote "The Cotter's Saturday Night." One can appropriate his line, "From scenes like these old Scotia's grandeur springs."

History proclaims repeatedly the value of home religion—the kind that gets into the daily life of people and voluntarily expresses itself in worship and in prayer. In 1848 when every throne in Europe was shaken or overturned, the Queen of England could walk and drive in safety. After a visit to that land M. Guizot said to Lord Shaftesbury, "I will tell you what has saved your empire. Not your police or army or statesmen. It was the deep, solemn religious atmosphere that is breathed over the whole people of England." It is now some years

since the Wall Street Journal made
a statement which it is still appropriate to recall. "What America
needs more than railway extension,
and Western irrigation, and a low
tariff, and a bigger wheat crop, and
a merchant marine, and a new navy,
is a revival of piety, the kind mother
and father used to have—piety that
counted it good business to stop for
daily family prayer before breakfast, right in the middle of the harvest; that quit field work a half
hour early Thursday night so as to
get the chores done and go to prayer
meeting. That's what we need now
to clean this country of the filth of
graft, and of greed, petty and big;
of worship of fine houses and big
lands and high office and grand
social functions." In later days the
late Woodrow Wilson pointed out

that the road away from revolution is found in the spirit of Christ and that civilization cannot survive materially unless it is redeemed spiritually.

2. "The Angelus" suggests that prayer is sometimes listening. It is meant to be a conversation, not a monologue. The attitude of some is "Hear, Lord, for thy servant speaketh," instead of "Speak, Lord; for thy servant heareth." From the distant church tower the bell summons to prayer in a sweet persuasiveness that cannot be resisted, in a language all can understand, in a gentle yet glorious eloquence from its metal lips, in a ministry that must melt the hardest heart and stir the finest emotions.

Science has made us understand we are in a vibrant universe. The radiophone has made this evident to multitudes. By this means we pick up messages otherwise undiscernible. The air is full of music. It is a symbol of those finer sensibilities of the soul by which communion is held with God's broadcasting station in the skies. We need to put out an aerial and tune in. This is the realm of prayer. By this listening process we get advance information and revelations of truth. Elijah heard the sound of an abundance of rain before he saw a single cloud in the sky. Jesus heard his Father's voice when the duller souls around him thought that it thundered. Do we besiege heaven with our complaints and requests or wait betimes and listen? It is not necessary to go to some shrine or altar, for the true worshipers are those who worship in spirit and in truth.

"If we live a life of prayer
God is present everywhere."

3. "The Angelus" suggests the relation of the church and prayer. The impulse to pray is native to the human heart. Temples, churches, cathedrals are an attempt to house this impulse. They reflect the experiences of life. The church's door is the portal to spiritual concepts; its walls rise in protection about the troubled soul, its windows let in the light of another world, its ceiling typifies the overarching mercy of God, and in its spire architecture leaps into poetry to express the aspirations of the heart. Jesus said, "My Father's house shall be called of all nations a house of prayer."

There are buildings for merchandise and learning and amusement, there are types of architecture that belong to certain centuries and peoples, but wherever we see a church amid the city's crowded traffic or along a country lane we recognize it as a House of Prayer.

But the function of the church is to send folks out into the fields, out into the highways, out to the market place, out to every task in the spirit of prayer. The church is not meant to monopolize the life of the spirit. It is meant to refresh and spiritualize every other activity in which we engage. Oh, ye who dwell in a house of bondage, turn to the House of Prayer.

THE MAN WITH THE HOE

Millet

THE MAN WITH THE HOE

When God made man it was from the dust of earth. When man's mortal remains are carried to their final resting place the pronouncement is made "Dust to dust." Is this attachment to the earth so close that it is impossible for us to arise and escape? The function of religion is to rescue the soul from slavery to the earth, to awaken man's spiritual nature and cause him to dwell in the consciousness of eternal values.

François Millet in his portrayal of "The Man With the Hoe" has given us a study in this struggle. Here is the stooped form of one who has made conquest with a grub hoe. He seeks a livelihood from an earth that seems unfriendly and reluctant.

He feels the exactions of that dictum
"In the sweat of thy face shalt
thou eat bread." His body has
suffered frost bite and sunburn. He
knows long hours and hard work and
loneliness. A peasant whose labor
has been exploited, leaving him with
scarce enough to satisfy his hunger,
the subject of economic discrimina-
tion, the victim of profiteers, he
stands in perplexity and in need, a
dull, sullen, and despairing man.

Edwin Markham has given us the
most illuminating interpretation of
this picture:

"Bowed by the weight of centuries he leans
  Upon his hoe and gazes on the ground,
  The emptiness of ages in his face,
  And on his back the burden of the world.
  Who made him dead to rapture and despair,
  A thing that grieves not and that never
      hopes,
  Stolid and stunned, a brother to the ox?

164

THE MAN WITH THE HOE

Who loosened and let down this brutal
    jaw?
Whose was the hand that slanted back his
    brow?
Whose breath blew out the light within
    this brain?

Is this the Thing the Lord God made and
    gave
To have dominion over sea and land;
To trace the stars and search the heavens
    for power;
To feel the passion of Eternity?
Is this the Dream He dreamed who shaped
    the suns
And pillared the blue firmament with light?
Down all the stretch of Hell to its last gulf
There is no shape more terrible than this—
More tongued with censure of the world's
    blind greed—
More filled with signs and portents for the
    soul—
More fraught with menace to the universe.
What gulfs between him and the seraphim:
Slave of the wheel of labor, what to him
Are Plato and the swing of Pleiades?

PICTURES THAT PREACH

What the long reaches of the peaks of song,
The rift of dawn, the reddening of the rose?
Through this dread shape the suffering ages
        look;
Time's tragedy is in that aching stoop;
Through this dread shape humanity be-
        trayed,
Plundered, profaned and disinherited,
Cries protest to the Judges of the World,
A protest that is also prophecy.

O masters, lords and rulers in all lands,
Is this the handiwork you give to God,
This monstrous thing distorted and soul-
        quenched?
How will you ever straighten up this shape;
Touch it again with immortality;
Give back the upward looking and the light;
Rebuild in it the music and the dream;
Make right the immemorial infamies,
Perfidious wrongs, immedicable woes?

O masters, lords and rulers in all lands,
How will the Future reckon with this Man?
How answer his brute question in that hour
When whirlwinds of rebellion shake the
        world?

THE MAN WITH THE HOE

How will it be with kingdoms and with
    kings—
With those who shaped him to the thing
    he is—
When this dumb Terror shall reply to God,
After the silence of the centuries?"[1]

The significance of all this for us
is the fact that to-day this "protest that is also prophecy" is a
prophecy in process of fulfillment.
This man with a hoe has straight-
ened up and there is a new light in
his eye. There are evidences in
some places that he has thrown
down his hoe and seized a torch and
a red flag. Certain nations have
already been visited by "whirlwinds
of rebellion" because of him. "Kingdoms and kings" and "those who
shaped him to the thing he is" have
fared ill in our time because he has

---

[1] Used by permission of author.

spoken out his resentment in both words and deeds. Many events in current history can only be interpreted or understood as we enter sympathetically into the viewpoint of the man who feels that he is "bowed by the weight of centuries" and has been made to carry "on his back the burden of the world."

In the early days of the Confederacy requests for an appropriate seal were made. A commission was appointed to consider the suggestions submitted. One which excited favor was the picture of a cotton bale on which a Negro lay asleep. It was shown to Jefferson Davis, who remarked with real concern in voice and manner, "But what will we do when he awakes?" To-day the sleeping Negro is awake. The enslaved and oppressed everywhere are waking. Their voices are heard in strident appeal and demand. What will we do? To study and understand this movement in modern society is imperative.

When the Declaration of Independence was signed, it was by men who felt they were escaping the masters of oppression. We are told that the great majority of these men were to be personally benefited by independence from England. They expected to secure an economic advantage for themselves by having a free country. This should not mitigate against their love of freedom or the sanctity of that patriotic ardor with which they acted. What they proposed for themselves they secured for those who should come after them. Equality of opportunity to work, to secure through initiative and industry the rewards of toil and the rights of property were written into our fundamental law and our philosophy of government. This conviction is stoutly fixed in the mind of the American citizen. But we are told to-day that great "interests" have secured power and that the political autocracy from which men once escaped is now displaced by a financial autocracy under which the laboring man is still made to suffer. The man with a hoe has been particularly clamorous in his protests and his answer is the Non-Partisan League. His purpose to secure relief is registered in electing State officials and congressional representatives who will do his will. He is thoroughly aroused. He is organized. Farmers could paralyze the country if they went on strike.

Society would suffer a knockout-hit below the belt.

The defect in the present situation concerning this man with a hoe is the fact that in America his mind has been addled with Russian poison. The cases of the European peasant and the American farmer are not analogous. Yet there are those who identify them. They read the resentment of toilers in other lands into their own mental attitude. They become inflamed and abusive when inventory would show that this great, fertile, plenteous America has been a friend furnishing opportunity, sustenance, independence, and prosperity manifold.

Here is a storm center into which have come many factors, an hour in history "when whirlwinds of rebellion shake the world" because the thing that Millet portrayed and Markham prophesied has transpired. It is a complex requiring patient study, self-control, good will.

Who has not felt the burden of weariness and toil? Who cannot sympathize with the man with the hoe? Who would not relieve the burden of the oppressed? Henry Ford has said in an interview that he conceived it as a part of his mission to take the burden from the backs of men and put it on machines. We are told that the cost of the Great War to the United States for one half year would put an automobile and tractor on every one of the six and one half million farms and leave six hundred million dollars for the improvement of good roads. If that were done, the man with a hoe would doubtless feel that his

Catch the inspiration of his motive. His purpose was to build the kingdom of God into the life of the world. Is there a higher motive for us? Motive determines value. The man with a hoe can cultivate or kill the growing harvest. The man with a torch can light the way or destroy. What are your motives? Such a question has power to strip the soul down to reality. Why are we here? What excuse have we for living? How do we justify our existence? Is there any reason why we should live another day? Are we measuring life in wealth or pleasure or ease—what? God is calling each of us to an allegiance of every power to the task to which Jesus was dedicated, to consecrate our talents and time to the mission yet unfulfilled to which he gave the last full measure of devotion.

day had come. But we cannot expect machines alone to do the world's work. The human factor always enters in. A false philosophy is abroad just now against which a warning may justly be sounded. Men are seeking legislation to correct evils that only industry can cure. Some folks think the government owes them a living and should step in and cover every financial loss they may sustain through poor investment or bad management. Too many are rendering a minimum of service for which they expect a maximum of wage. The problem in our time is not so much one of labor as one of leisure. The commandment is "Six days shalt thou labor," as well as "Remember the Sabbath day, to keep it holy." No man is entitled to one day of rest until he has earned it with six days of work. The man roosting on an iron rail across the street from an employment office and the denizen of the fashionable club yawning with ennui amid soft cushions both fall under this indictment. Society should develop a new contempt for idlers—both the idle rich and the idle poor. The man with some useful occupation is to be congratulated and not pitied. If you have to work do not complain, but rejoice.

> "The toil of brain or heart or hand
> Is man's appointed lot,
> He who God's call can understand
> Will work and murmur not.
> Toil is no thorny crown of pain
> Bound round man's brow for sin.
> True souls from it all strength may gain
> High manliness to win."

Jesus was a toiler. He was a car-

penter and wage-earner. He knew hunger and hard work. He understood the lot of the poor. He had compassion on the multitudes.

Catch the inspiration of his example. How industrious he was! We hear Him saying "I must be about my Father's business," "My Father worketh hitherto, and I work," "I must work the works of him that sent me, while it is day," "I have finished the work which thou gavest me to do." He worked to the point of exhaustion. Once they took ship on Galilee and he slept serenely on the hard deck while wind and wave wrought such havoc as to arouse a panic of fear in the disciples. He was tired and unconscious of the peril until they wakened him, and then he imparted the peace of own heart to the sea.

day had come. But we cannot
expect machines alone to do the
world's work. The human factor
always enters in. A false philosophy
is abroad just now against which a
warning may justly be sounded.
Men are seeking legislation to correct evils that only industry can
cure. Some folks think the government owes them a living and should
step in and cover every financial loss
they may sustain through poor investment or bad management. Too
many are rendering a minimum of
service for which they expect a
maximum of wage. The problem in
our time is not so much one of
labor as one of leisure. The commandment is "Six days shalt thou
labor," as well as "Remember the
Sabbath day, to keep it holy." No
man is entitled to one day of rest

until he has earned it with six days of work. The man roosting on an iron rail across the street from an employment office and the denizen of the fashionable club yawning with ennui amid soft cushions both fall under this indictment. Society should develop a new contempt for idlers—both the idle rich and the idle poor. The man with some useful occupation is to be congratulated and not pitied. If you have to work do not complain, but rejoice.

"The toil of brain or heart or hand
  Is man's appointed lot,
He who God's call can understand
  Will work and murmur not.
Toil is no thorny crown of pain
  Bound round man's brow for sin.
True souls from it all strength may gain
  High manliness to win."

Jesus was a toiler. He was a carpenter and wage-earner. He knew hunger and hard work. He understood the lot of the poor. He had compassion on the multitudes.

Catch the inspiration of his example. How industrious he was! We hear Him saying "I must be about my Father's business," "My Father worketh hitherto, and I work," "I must work the works of him that sent me, while it is day," "I have finished the work which thou gavest me to do." He worked to the point of exhaustion. Once they took ship on Galilee and he slept serenely on the hard deck while wind and wave wrought such havoc as to arouse a panic of fear in the disciples. He was tired and unconscious of the peril until they wakened him, and then he imparted the peace of his own heart to the sea.

Catch the inspiration of his motive. His purpose was to build the kingdom of God into the life of the world. Is there a higher motive for us? Motive determines value. The man with a hoe can cultivate or kill the growing harvest. The man with a torch can light the way or destroy. What are your motives? Such a question has power to strip the soul down to reality. Why are we here? What excuse have we for living? How do we justify our existence? Is there any reason why we should live another day? Are we measuring life in wealth or pleasure or ease—what? God is calling each of us to an allegiance of every power to the task to which Jesus was dedicated, to consecrate our talents and time to the mission yet unfulfilled to which he gave the last full measure of devotion.